The Uneaten Carrots of Atonement

Also by Diane Lockward

Temptation by Water
What Feeds Us
Eve's Red Dress
Greatest Hits 1997 - 2010 (chapbook)
Against Perfection (chapbook)

The Crafty Poet: A Portable Workshop

The Uneaten Carrots
of
Atonement

Diane Lockward

Wind Publications

Copyright © 2016 by Diane Lockward
Printed in the United States of America.
All rights reserved.
No part of this book may be reproduced in any manner,
except for brief quotations embodied in critical articles
or reviews.

Wind Publications
4 Midvale Avenue
West Caldwell, NJ 07006

ISBN: 978-0-9969871-1-0
LCCN: 2015919935

First Edition

Cover art: Brian Rumbolo

for Abbigale and Coley

Contents

My Arty *Ars Poetica:* A Cento   / 3

One

Original Sin   / 7
I Want to Save the Trees   / 9
How Heavy the Snow   / 11
The Phone Call   / 12
Dreaming to Lionel Richie's "Dancing on the
    Ceiling"   / 14
The Gift of a Rat   / 15
Thinking Like a Buddhist   / 16
How I Dumped You   / 18
Knot-Tying   / 19
Shopping at the Short Hills Mall   / 20
The Color of Magic   / 22

Two

The Instincts of a Dog   / 27
After   / 28
All Night Awake, My Innards Gone Awry   / 30
In Defense of the Cashew   / 31
We Were Such a Fine Plum Pudding   / 33
How Many Times Did They Need to Be Told?   / 34
Warnings   / 36
In My Bones   / 38
The Morphology of Mushrooms   / 40
Nesting   / 41
"Why yellow makes me sad"   / 42

Three

The Wrong Monkey   / 47
Sweet Images   / 49

For the Love of Avocados   / 51
Two-Door Mailbox with Gin   / 52
The Pull of Bones   / 54
August 11: Morning Prelude   / 55
The Seasons of a Long Marriage   / 56
Losing Daylight   / 57
Morning Walk   / 59

Four
Eminent Domain   / 63
The Third Egg   / 64
Preservation   / 65
By the side of the road   / 66
The Light Sets the Record Straight   / 67
Why I Read True Crime Books   / 68
My New Boyfriend Covers Me Like a Floral Scarf   / 70
Your Beard, I Love It Not   / 72
Untying the Knot: A Sonnenizio   / 74
For the Chocolate Tasters   / 75
A Polemic for Pink   / 76

Five
An Epistemology of Promiscuity   / 81
In My Yard, the Bones of Trees   / 83
Sinkholes   / 84
Your Blue Shirt   / 86
Where Feathers Go When They Fall   / 87
Coloring   / 89
The Morning After   / 90
Pity the Poor Fortune Cookie Writer His Muse   / 91
Signs   / 93
And Life Goes On As It Has Always Gone On   / 94

Acknowledgments   / 97
About the Author   / 101

The beginning of atonement is the sense of its necessity.

—Lord Byron

. . . carrots are often inefficient.

—Brian Galle, *The Tragedy of the Carrots*

My Arty *Ars Poetica:* A Cento

> *. . . poets pretend they don't know anything about
> their own writing processes and get arty and mysterious
> when asked about it . . .*
> —Kenny Williams, *Rattle* Contributors' Notes

I was raised in Abilene. More chickens than humans down
there. Worked construction, captured moments,

created stories. It was solitary work. Below the Blue
Ridge Mountains loved a man with a gnarly beard.

I'm pathologically nice. My brother has perfect pitch.
I write to one-up him. I use an assumed voice, am

learning the names of things, and can't stop—I have
obsessive-compulsive disorder. Once threatened

in a beer joint in Arkansas. Spent hours among tall bolts
of fabric, tins of loose buttons, and leftover notions. My

words are knotted twine. Call it a reinvention. Walked
a peach orchard alone at night and saw the Milky Way,

felt freighted with a sense of mortality. Sleep sounds
like a pleasant dream. Cut my musical teeth in the jungle.

This is my singing, my attempt to insulate the violence,
to euphemize the shooting. Misery is universal. The only

math I know is balance. This is my way of preserving
memory. I make beautiful the moments of terror.

One

Original Sin

When Karen told my father I'd pulled off
my rabbit's tail, he asked, *Did you?* And I
said, *Yes,* though in truth it was Karen

who'd grabbed the tail and tugged and tugged
until it came loose in her hand. My father
slapped me hard, said I'd been cruel,

and asked why I'd done it. I confessed I didn't
know and took the strap for Karen's crime.
In the days and weeks that followed, I never

questioned or accused Karen, and she never
acknowledged what she'd done or apologized.
We did not speak of her lie, or mine.

One morning at summer's end I found my rabbit
dead in her pen. Her sweet body, already stiff,
lay among the uneaten carrots of atonement,

and where the tail had been, a small red circle,
an accusing eye, reminded me of my deception.
I wondered then and wonder still why I took

the blame for hurting the pet I'd loved. I only know
that once Karen said I'd done it and my father
looked at me as if I had, I was guilty,

as guilty as those unbaptized babies
in Purgatory. I must have understood even then
that I'd been born bad and the only reason

I hadn't yanked off my rabbit's tail was because
Karen got it first. Some part of me, the part
already destined for Hell, had wanted

that soft talisman that promised luck, wanted it
in my own hand, and wished I'd moved faster.

I Want to Save the Trees

That's why I water them, a holy communion without wafer
or wine, and why I eat vegetables

shaped like trees—upside down green peppers,
mushrooms, broccoli stalks with dozens of florets—

and why I abhor my neighbors for their crimes—
the endless buzz of chainsaws and in the backyard

logs piled up like corpses after a massacre.
I pamper my trees, indulge them in birdfeeders

and the joy of feathers and fur. I love the green
of leaves and the flying fluff. So easy to overlook

the clogged gutters, to admire the longevity
of trees, their fidelity, and willingness to stick

it out. On my knees, I beg the oak's forgiveness.
If I'd known that the filthy knife wielder was rotten

as a diseased Dutch Elm, I would not have let him
shove in his blade and carve a heart into the bark,

his initials and mine forever locked inside,
my tree wounded, forever tattooed like a prisoner.

Nor would I sit in this garden now, surrounded
by peonies, each pink bloom unfolding a thin line

of ants like a single black hair from my lover's groin.
As light streams through the foliage, I pray hard

for the transmogrification of that wound into the face
of Jesus. I curse my faithless lover with his heart

rot and his ring of lies, his roots weak and shallow
as the willow's uprooted in last winter's storm.

How Heavy the Snow

It weighs down the burning bushes that burn
no more, loads the porch railings with more
than they can bear. Even the tiny holes
of window screens fill with the color of absence.

It billows and blows like sheets on a line,
builds a shroud around the house,
covers the ground with a blanket of white
unmarked by footprints.

As if by conjury, wild turkeys appear,
at least two dozen in single file. Almost terrifying
the way they spread across the yard,
an army invading from a foreign land. Strange,

ugly birds, their long, arrogant necks black
and greasy, bellies distended. Out of season,
hungry and desperate, they swivel their heads
like periscopes and peck the seedless snow.

Only their footsteps remain,
each no bigger than a child's, evidence
only that once they were here
and then disappeared.

The Phone Call

It happens on a morning
much like any other—
ginger tea, a bowl of oatmeal,
and English Muffins,
split and slathered
with peach preserves.
Your husband's upstairs shaving,
his face covered in white foam
when the phone rings,
and suddenly you're racing
up the stairs, breakfast
turning cold, the morning
crushed like a sheet of tin.
You reach the top, breathless,
and there's your husband
coming out of the bathroom,
clean and fresh,
smelling of mint and lime,
his strong arms around you,
no words at all—
he already knows what's wrong.
This is the tipping point,
the crux of your marriage.
Beyond this hour, this moment,
nothing will ever be the same.
You will stick together, moving
like two shadows, the sorrow
between you a cord stretched
from one to the other,
the life you build
like a house, one room closed,
cordoned off as in a museum,
behind the rope,

the furniture of your grief
while downstairs the kettle
boils and shrieks,
its whistle calling you back
to the business of breathing in
and breathing out.

Dreaming to Lionel Richie's "Dancing on the Ceiling"

I float up and up, my arms now wings,
and back to the room where I once
was a girl, sent to bed early while my
parents figured out how to end
their marriage. Suspended like a bat
from the ceiling, vantage point
phenomenal, I see the white eyelet
curtains being eyed by my cat. Her first
heat and wild with desire, she howls
like a madwoman, leaps from the floor,
and with her claws pulls and pulls until
the curtains hang like strands of linguine.
I see the bureau, top drawer minus
the money my father stole while I slept,
and the bottom drawer, my blood
on the edge, a scar already forming
on my lip. And the chair that hides
the monster who comes in the night
to enter my dreams. In the closet,
the red taffeta dress I can't wear
because my father says red is a color
for a whore. I see the bed where a girl
lays dreaming, seeds inside her
churning, that girl dreaming a man,
the two of them embraced in a waltz,
long before the flamenco's fierce
yearning and pulsing hips, long before
the slither of the tango and intertwined
limbs, before the arrogant paso doble,
its separation and attack, its quick,
sharp steps like flint against steel,
her red satin dress in flames, her red
leather spikes setting the floor on fire.

The Gift of a Rat

A broken creature at my feet   dropped
by the predatory cat who'd stalked him
and quietly crouched   stationary as a bush

her whiskers stiff   her pink tongue saltier
as she bided until the rat was deep into his
cheese   a chunk nudged from trash   balm

to nights of hunger when hunger hurts most
his front paws clutching the bright cheddar
and twitching with desire   he sniffs it again

and again   petite kisses   playful and eager
whiskers washed   now dusted with cheese
as he nibbles and nibbles   and in that moment

of rapture   the cat begins to move   one foot
in front of the other   seamlessly   like a time
lapse film   and she pounces   grabs the rat

by his neck   sinks in her teeth   and though
he struggles   she won't let go   impales him
with her claws and punctures again and again

until the rat goes limp   tail dangling like a worm
the cheese   his last supper   left unfinished
and the cat releases her grip   nibbles the cheese

slowly   one lick at a time   this precious treasure
this topaz   this nugget of gold   and she nibbles
until her hunger is appeased   stuffs the rat

into the small purse of her mouth   carries it home
her trophy   her gift   her declaration of love
and drops it at my feet   Even in this there is beauty

Thinking Like a Buddhist

Among the nasturtiums, a dead grackle, its feathers
obsidian in sunlight. Something moves like a shadow—

the busy work of flies, green with iridescent wings.
They dig in like Vikings into a suckling pig. The bird's

dead so he doesn't care, but I want to smash those flies
that have no respect for the recently fallen, and I

want to know how this particular bird happened to fall.
Did he plummet mid-flight when his time was up?

Had he flown like an idiot into a window, bounced off,
and plopped into my nasturtiums? The only other dead

birds I've ever seen were at the bottom of a cage—
parakeets I neglected in my youth—or robins my

hubristic cat carried home as gifts. I think of the paucity
of dead birds, and I wonder, Where do birds go to die?

Why isn't the earth littered with wrens, their wings folded,
eyes like glass beads? Why has no jogger ever been

pelted with deceased sparrows? Shouldn't dead crows
be blocking the entrance to the Shop-Rite, blue jays lying

on highways? How do birds arrange their deaths in places
so obscure no one ever finds the bodies, like those corpses

dumped by mobsters into vacant lots and construction sites?
And why the desire for anonymity in death? Such are my

thoughts as I stand in my garden among blossoms of orange
and yellow, witness to this mountainless sky burial, the green

iridescence of hundreds of wings, the mad flutter of hunger,
the frenzied dance of thieves come to ransack a mansion.

How I Dumped You

I cast you off the way a cicada wiggles out of its husk,
a vacated hotel on the bark of a tree. The way a snake
moults, its skin somebody else's belt now.
Like the extraction of a bad molar, rotten at the root,
and though the hole bled and required seven days
of diarrhea-inducing antibiotics, it filled with a pearl.
As a baby loses its first hair, the fuzz gathered like tufts
of tumbleweed, the mother getting used to loss in small
bites, I lost you hair by hair. Dropped you like a diseased
branch ripped from a tree, broken in pieces, tinder
into the fire. Quietly, like a bird feather, while I flew south
without you, my wings flapping faster and faster,
the feather an amulet, a talisman, a warning. I flicked you
off like a flake of dandruff. Oh Christ! how you made me
itch. I dug in and picked you out like a scab, opened
the wound again and again. Yes, I am scarred. Because
no patch could repair you, because no landfill could
hold you, I dumped you like an old tire onto the highway.
I violated a local ordinance and hurled you like a bagful
of dog-doo onto someone else's yard, tossed you like
watermelon rind after a picnic, like a brown banana peel,
like a used Kleenex, like a dead chipmunk. I scraped you
from the sole of my sneaker like a wad of chewed-up gum.
Deleted you from the dictionary, a dated word, obsolete
and rootless. I'll never need your name again. I became
an oak and held to the bark like a cicada, my lacey wings
grown hard as bone. I tossed you out like a peanut shell.

Knot-Tying

I am learning the intricate art of tying knots,
    not delicate ones from strings and ribbons,
but knots from ropes no knives can cut—

    nylon, true and strong, manila braided
from hemp, and lariat rope that resists
    a strain by pulling tighter and tighter.

I want to master the lark's head, so firm
    it restrains what it holds from flight,
and the bowline whose noose never slides,

jams, or fails—it gets the job done—
    and the cat's paw useful in hoisting a hook.
I want to master the over- and underhand

of intertwined loops. But not the ease and release
    of the clove hitch. I want knots beautiful
like lace and knots for rescue—the figure-eight,

    the water knot, and the double loop.
Let my fingers master the slip knot,
    the diamond knot, and the shroud knot

from which no one slips. I want knots
    elaborate as a bird's nest, knots to weave
a hammock held fast between trees,

knots that hold their weight, that won't come
    undone, knots to make a lasso to bring back
what runs. I want the single Gordian knot

so complicated no man could ever
    unravel it, the knot strong enough to hitch
a halter to what's wild and tame it.

Shopping at the Short Hills Mall

I walked into a store and bought a new husband.
The old one had conked out and was minus
irreplaceable parts. The store had advertised
a new, improved model, and they took trade-ins
which was attractive as I wanted to eke out
one last bit of value from the dud I'd dragged in,
plus now I wouldn't have to worry about disposing
of him in an ecologically responsible manner.
I looked at several models and lingered over one
that came fully loaded. I wasn't going to settle this time.
The salesman explained each feature
and made this potential husband sound comprehensible
and easy to use. He demonstrated how to operate him
with a remote control, a device I'd seen but never held.
He showed me the right button to push to keep him clean
and sober. He showed me how to sanitize the mouth.
There was a button for tricks, one for special effects,
and one to get colored lights going. The salesman
promised that this model could do house repairs
and was good with his hands. Of course, he attempted
an upsell. For an extra $50, this husband would sing
in the shower without restraint. And when I turned
him on, he'd do the same for me. I checked to be sure
the heart was in the right place and appropriately soft.
My old husband had worried about the thickness
of his heart. I'd worried about the hardness.
Of course, the new one would love me—a feature
common to all the new models and something,
the salesman assured me, I'd soon get used to
and wonder how I'd ever lived without it.
I put my money on the counter, a year's worth
of groceries, but knew I'd never starve again.
The salesman said if I could wait he'd charge up
my new husband. I agreed as I seemed to have lost

the knack and had already waited for years.
I passed the time imagining a night of kisses,
two arms around me like a warm coat.
I handed over my old husband and felt him
shake just a bit. As I walked out with my new husband,
I heard the old one calling my name, like a song, like a prayer.

The Color of Magic

Red of the raspberry, its drupelets
    a nest of sexual seeds,
        and the music, pepper hot and red,
foot-tapping, foot-stomping music,
    wail of the sax,
        red satin dress sparking flames,
          and the red-bellied snake
    on your shoulders,
    our hands clapping belief
in some unholy act, some magic trick—
rabbit out of the hat,
    coin behind the ear,
        scarf from the sleeve,
your red-headed lady disassembled, reassembled.

Give us illusion, optical and otherwise,
the miracle of belief, tiny O of surprise.

We want everything red—
cranberry juice,
    maraschino cherry, that jewel in a jar,
        and red velvet cake,
           poison spot on the belly,
      taste of the music,
    your cape's silk lining
flashing in waves of light.

We want the pigeon-blood ruby, fire on the finger,
    and the ruby-throated hummingbird
        that flies upside down,
           mates midair,
      and vanishes,
    the cardinal always in contention
with his own reflection,
    but when he commits,

     commits forever,
and the tree frog,
   his red eyes lit up
     like lightbulbs and bulging
       as if perpetually amazed.

Transform our tomatoes into the liquid velvet
    of the Bloody Mary.
      Let it slide down our throats,
   scarlet red and slippery
as any snake, hot as jazz.

Two

The Instincts of a Dog

Sometimes to sidestep an obligation or invitation, I say, *I have to take the dog to the vet*, though the dog's been dead for twenty years and wasn't even mine—it was my brother's. I like the sound of those words—*I have to take the dog to the vet*. It's what responsible, compassionate people say, the kind who go to wakes and parties, the kind who attend to a dog's needs and don't mind being seen walking with a bagful of turds.

When I was a kid, a German shepherd named *Freund* attacked my little brother and bit his private parts. A passing milkman rescued him. He carried my brother home and dropped him off like a quart of milk. True, it was my brother the dog attacked, not me, but we had no dessert that night because my mother was hysterical and could not stop crying. She bought my brother a dachshund to help him get over his fear of dogs. That elongated mutt vomited worms on the furniture, peed all over the house, and sunk his teeth into my ankles when he walked between my brother and me.

Even then I preferred to walk alone, dogless, and unaccosted as I did today, enjoying the greenery and yellow daffodils, the peace of my aloneness. I sat awhile in the park and watched a small child with his mother. They stood by the lake preparing to launch a boat made of popsicle sticks and Styrofoam, a blue cotton sail mounted to the top. The boy kneeled and, holding tight to a string, set his boat in the water. As it drifted farther and farther, he became afraid and dropped the string. His boat foundered and sunk, its blue sail waving goodbye, goodbye. The boy began to weep and howl.

It was the same sound my brother made the day the leash slipped out of his fingers and his dog disappeared, the same howling all that day and for many days after, his small hand in mine as we searched the neighborhood, his face red, his cries just that high-pitched and desperate, his lungs gasping for air.

After

Hours before you wake, before
you remember, as you do each morning,

what you are afraid of, before you wake
into the strange country

that lives inside you, sweaty with fear,
the fear you might feel crossing the border

from Mexico, not knowing where the bullets
will fly from, chanting like a Buddhist,

*You're okay, you're okay, nothing
has happened,* your morning mantra,

what will hoist you out of bed
and plunge you into morning

as into an ice-cold lake, what will pull
your crumpled pink gown over your knees,

your legs, as the sweat turns cold,
and you practice breathing,

like an aphasic learning to speak again,
alarm blaring as it does each day,

though you lie awake most nights,
time to get up, get up, to push against

the weight on your chest, the crush
of Winston's black dog—*good dog,*

you coax, *bad dog,* patting his haunches,
holding his chain as he drags you to the edge

of the lake, as you put one foot in the water,
then the other, and wade up to your neck

as he splashes and wags his tail,
pulling you down like a sack of stones.

All Night Awake, My Innards Gone Awry

That cistern of bilge and bulge, cesspool of bad ideas
a hornet's nest, my black ball of fear
      buzzing even after the beekeeper's extraction

temporary housing for sweet drifters and grifters
my boiler room, its furnace all flames, night shift worker
      a devil man who shovels and scrapes

my round pot of earth, seed place of poisonous growth
a crucible, alchemical sludge skimmed off the top

crockpot slow-cooking a stew of confusion
my soup pot simmering chowder while I stir

that petri dish, lab experiment gone awry
      dozens of eggs, all broken

that hanging feeder stuffed with indigestible peanuts
      woodpeckers pecking, the empty shells left behind

my medicine ball that makes me sick
my crystal ball foretelling trouble, the call that shatters
      glass, shatters crystal, shatters everything

the abandoned mine no canary could survive in
sinkhole that opens each night and swallows me whole

my bird's nest, stolen by another
      cowbird, cuckoo, mourning dove
fishbowl without a fish—did I like a guppy eat my young

This is Detroit, my bankrupt metropolis, ghost town
      vacant building in a condemned neighborhood
        room without a renter, a shut-down factory
      a motorless city

In Defense of the Cashew

> *It all started when I tried a cashew . . .*
> —Elizabeth Bishop

Confined to bed for weeks, her flesh distorted,
like someone beaten or burned,
she railed against the obscenity of the cashew.

And yet she'd reached out and taken that nut,
curled like a baby's ear moon,
a child sleeping.

Seed stuck to the bottom of the cashew apple,
fruit of a tree, the old story again,
a different kind of disaster.

She cursed its bulbous top, narrow conclusion,
freak of a nut, like a hunchbacked letter C,
dislodged kidney, miniature boxing glove.

Brazilian delicacy, a luxury, reputed beneficial
for the heart, near-death for Elizabeth.

Impossible to refuse the crooked finger,
so easy to take what's offered,
so hard to turn away from the misshapen moon.

What the cashew started her new lover
completed, the two of them lost in the lushness
of Brazil, love ripening like an exotic fruit.

Did she perceive the split down the middle,
the subtle fracture, the way the world
sometimes cracks open?

Clenched fist, apostrophe, signal of absence,
the desperation of the fetal position,
love grown more fatal than any cashew.

We Were Such a Fine Plum Pudding

Temptation it is
to read your spread palm,
the abbreviated lifeline and bad fortune,
as palm to palm we are no more,
nor plum to plum.

Such a fine pudding we made,
the long slow steam to perfection,
the struck match, the two of us drenched
in cognac and served in a blaze.
And oh! the very texture of us,
so dark we were almost black,
and dear God! so sinfully rich,
currants inside us plump and sweet,
and clotted cream like a moat around the base.

Yet the proof was in us—
at the heart, not a coin hidden, but a snake coiled.
The old story again—paradise at hand,
a man, a woman, a fruited tree,
only plum this time, perhaps for variety,
or so we thought—in truth, merely the illusion
of plums, our pudding misnamed and false,
overbaked and ruined—
my moist plum dried up, your poor plum
shriveled, a plumless pudding after all.

How Many Times Did They Need to Be Told?

He forgot to always wear clean underwear.
She forgot about buns in the oven.

She should have been resistant to the power of blue—
left it for the sky and the aquamarines.

He should have studied cause and effect.
She should have danced all night.

Couldn't she for once have listened to her mother?
Why'd they have bananas in their ears?

It might have been the fruit of his biceps.
It might have been his passion for pistachios.

Couldn't she have eschewed his red shells?
Couldn't he have kept his filthy fingers out of her pie?

He should have pursued his own manifest destiny.
But how could he when he couldn't read a map?

And for Pete's sake and all that's holy, why hadn't he hit
the brakes, why not just in the knick of time?

They should have paid attention to the lunar cycle.
They should have observed the consistency of tides.

Why'd they go to school if not to learn how to count?
Why'd they dive headfirst into the deep end of the ocean?

They should be learning disco, swirling under a mirror ball,
wearing red satin Saturday night fever shirts

not awash in white, such a ghostly shade of pale,
no leap of faith, only the moon to jump over.

Maybe they'd be laughing like kids again,
like they still believed in luck, like they still believed in magic.

Warnings

Barney picked up the dead turtle, carried it
to the side of the road, and dangled it
by the tail in an upside down death dance.

We'd all been warned not to touch turtles
and not to mess with dead things,
but Barney never listened to grownups
and wasn't afraid of anything.

We'd seen him jump out of trees and throw
rocks at the O'Days' German shepherd.
He let bees crawl on his arms and didn't flinch,
not even when stung.

My father said Barney was too dumb to know
any better. My mother said that's what happens
when a boy's father hangs himself.

Barney dropped the turtle in the gravel.
One by one, we circled round and took turns
poking it with sticks.

None of us wanted to touch it with our fingers,
but Barney stroked the legs, the webbed feet,
the knife-sharp ridges of the mouth,
then licked his fingers and tasted death.

He moved the pad of his index finger across
the ancient markings of the shell as if reading
Braille, or memorizing a secret code—
a disciple learning the mystery of shells.

He grabbed a rock, raised his arm, and smashed
and smashed what was already long gone.
The rest of us ran home, afraid of what we'd seen—
inside that stony carapace, something moved.

In My Bones

    Through
   my nose,
  downstream
 into my throat,
a salmon swims
in my bones.
She navigates
the damaged
 ecosystem of my
  body, slips inside
  porous bones.
    Like an engineer
   fixing a faulty dam,
  she lays her eggs
 in the holes, the
hollow redds.
    All night I feel her
   undulations, the
  arching and
 reaching of back
and belly. I move
with the flapping
of her tail. Her
voice bubbles up
to the surface.
My ears swoosh
with water and
syllables. I hear her
calling her unborn
as once I called
my own. Pink with
 the oily ooze of
  salmon, her feathery
   flesh, and wild with
    desire for fresh water,

I swim upstream,
 against the current,
  through rapids
   and estuaries,
    as after long
     absence,
      I push for
       home.

The Morphology of Mushrooms

When my young son asks, *What's a mushroom?*
I tell him his face, his belly, his thighs.
I touch each spongy part of him with my finger.
He is deep into Wonderland, knows Alice
and the caterpillar, and hungers for more.
I give him edible fungus and nibble a toe.
I give him raised on a farm or wild in the forest.
Nourished by worms and redolent of iron.
I give him the fruiting body, spore-bearing and fleshy.
And under the dome, a network of blade-like gills
delicate as lace, fragile as a spider's web.
Squat tree, rubber umbrella, one-legged stool.
And on the lawn, ephemeral as a magic trick—
here in the morning, then the swift farewell.
I give him fairy ring, porcini, hen-of-the-woods.
Food for royalty. Ancient promise of immortality.
I do not give him atomic plume, or the locket,
mist of death cap hidden inside like a drop
of perfume. One dab on the lips, a different kind
of goodbye. Tonight, I slip the music of mushrooms
into his mouth—*chanterelle, portobello, morel.*

Nesting

Outside our window, a robin perched
in last year's nest, a scraggly bundle

tightly tucked behind the light fixture
and dangling sticks and strings.

You came to look, both of us surprised
to see a robin in an abandoned nest—

like a vagrant in a condemned building.
When she flew out, we saw a new nest

inside the old, last year's broken shells
buried under the new abode, bracing it

like a foundation of crushed stone,
and I thought how it has been like that

for us, building a new life inside the old,
how we have woven something new

out of fragments,
what we'd thought ruined, somehow

salvaged, the ghost of the old nest
always shadowing the new one,

as next to me, a man with silver hair,
while on the other side of the glass,

the girl I once was, the boy I once knew,
their faces still unbroken,

behind them, the apparition of a child,
his eyes sun-lit, his hair thick and dark.

"Why yellow makes me sad"

—Geico commercial

O! the paradox of lemons,
persistence of dandelions,
coins snatched from behind the magician's ear,
goldfinches that feed upside down,
snow to be avoided but marked as such,
and those freaks in the garden, sunflowers,
the coward's streak, the light that cautions,
line that can't be crossed,
the sun and sometimes the vacillating moon,
banana peels before they turn brown,
goldenrod with its frantic sneezing,
grilled cheese sandwiches, American and cheddar,
and yellow beyond reason, Anne Gregory's hair,

fall leaves, summer wheat, and corn in season,
mustard, saffron, and a whiff of sulfur,
indecisive emblem of hope, happiness, and deceit,
hazard signs, hard hats, and crime scene tape,
mourning clothes in Egypt,
fruit of the pineapple inside its prickly hide,
zucchinis, peppers, and geocentric onions,
the man who runs, yellowbellied and lily-livered,
ribbon tied around a tree when someone's missing,
teeth when they grow old,
journalism and egg yolks,
yellow-shafted flicker, yellowfin tuna,
peridot, topaz, and diamond,
ménage à trois with red and blue,

a kind of fever and its vector, the mosquito,
yellow jackets buzzing in forsythia,
crocus, tulips, and the rose of Texas,
school bus, taxicab, the Beatles' submarine,

Picasso's jug and his woman's hair,
penalty flag in football,
emergency vehicles by the side of the road,

Coldplay's song, everything he did for her, yellow,
Mountain Dew and Galliano,
the hills of California in a certain kind of light,
amber glow of memory,
color of terror, every phone call that comes in the night,
color that comes unbidden when I have called for blue,
the wheel broken, the spot empty and desolate,
blue without its complementary color.

Three

The Wrong Monkey

> *Nine Snow Monkeys Escape from Oregon Animal Testing Lab*
> —Alex Felsinger, *Planetsave*

When the guard forgot to lock the cage,
they'd snatched as many bananas
as they could carry and, like prisoners
seeking freedom, hopped the fence.
Hope lay in the leaf-covered branches of trees.

Notices went out: *Primates on the Run.*
Pictures were posted on telephone poles:
Have you seen these monkeys?
Anonymous callers reported monkeys at the mall,
monkeys on the university campus,
monkeys near the railroad tracks.

Soon an apple-assisted capture and eight monkeys
were back behind bars.

The head vet said, *I think they had a good time.
I think they enjoyed the sunshine.*
Describing the one monkey still at large, he warned,
*If you find a monkey wearing a wool cap,
that's the wrong monkey.*

Security is tightened, guards retrained,
trees downed, the old fence monkey-proofed.

To discourage recidivism, the captured monkeys
receive peanuts and caramels.
They spend their days eating their treats,
grooming each other, and hitting the bars.

They dream of when they'd dared to run
and turned their small, ruddy faces
to the sun. They dream of leaves.
They dream of needles and yarn.
They are learning to knit.

Sweet Images

The skinny girl inside her
dreams of slipping into a sleek silk shirt
matched up with a pencil-thin, skin-tight skirt,

but in her waking hours, the brownie
of her dreams, filled with naughty pieces
of chocolate and topped with fudge so creamy

it slides across her tongue,
so delicious it would be impossible, even wrong
to resist—her flesh is ample but not that strong.

She knows what it is to fall—
31 flavors of ice cream and she wants them all.
Like Alice, she hears each confection calling,

Eat me! A modern-day temptation, a snake
coiled in every cookie and cake.
She curses the patisserie and the bakery,

the almond-filled croissants, the meringues,
her tortured taste buds, and the hunger pangs
that cut her, sharper than the reptile's fangs.

But that interior girl, she has desires,
too. Another kind of hunger burns like fire—
to be svelte like the women she admires

in magazines and movies, women who dine
on lettuce and sip a glass of wine,
who wave away the dessert tray and do not pine

for cheesecake and tiramisu, its rum-soaked layers
of lady fingers pressed together in perverted prayer,
each finger crooked, inviting her into the caloric lair.

Rapacious as a dope fiend, she craves sugar,
whipped cream, pecan pie, and fabrics that hug her
hips without dimples or mounds of blubber.

She envisions herself in glossy photographs,
her hair wind-tossed, sweet words and laughter,
a bottle of Chardonnay, a shared bowl of roughage.

For the Love of Avocados

I sent him from home hardly more than a child.
Years later, he came back loving avocados.
In the distant kitchen where he'd flipped burgers
and tossed salads, he'd mastered how to prepare

the pear-shaped fruit. He took a knife and plied
his way into the thick skin with a bravado
and gentleness I'd never seen in him. He nudged
the halves apart, grabbed a teaspoon and carefully

eased out the heart, holding it as if it were fragile.
He took one half, then the other of the armadillo-
hided fruit and slid his spoon where flesh edged
against skin, working it under and around, sparing

the edible pulp. An artist working at an easel,
he filled the center holes with chopped tomatoes.
The broken pieces, made whole again, merged
into two reconstructed hearts, a delicate and rare

surgery. My boy who'd gone away angry and wild
had somehow learned how to unclose
what had once been shut tight, how to urge
out the stony heart and handle it with care.

Beneath the rind he'd grown as tender and mild
as that avocado, its rubies nestled in peridot,
our forks slipping into the buttery texture
of unfamiliar joy, two halves of what we shared.

Two-Door Mailbox with Gin

Inside the back door,
a half-empty martini glass
some wandering drunk
must have left behind,
taken one last swig,
and slipped out the front.
The rim had no lipstick,
the clear glass uncracked,
squeezed between batches
of coupons and catalogs.
It held an inch of gin
and the small sword
of a toothpick.
The stem was intact,
so I could take a drink
if I wanted. If I dared.
I wondered whose lips
had touched the rim,
whose fingers had lifted
the glass, what sorrows
had sunk to the bottom,
nestled like extra olives,
if some lost reveler,
tired of drinking alone
and desperate to get home,
had meant to leave
some kind of message,
some call for help,
if my mother had come back
from being dead,
come for one last drink
or to apologize,
my mother with her ruby lips
and painted nails.

I sniffed for the scent
of *Muguet des Bois*,
but it was already
the morning after,
and whatever drunk
had passed my way was gone,
leaving this fragile memento
among the darkness, the bills,
and the pile of bad news.

The Pull of Bones

What you are now we used to be;
what we are now you will be . . .
    —Inscription on the wall of the Capuchin Crypt

We mingled among headstones, mausoleums,
and plaque-lined rows. Impossible to explain
the lure of bones, compulsion of dirt and the dead,

all that whiteness underground, an invisible force
pulling us in, and the voices, they called to us,
sung to us, sweet as Sirens' song and just as hard

to resist. We went unbound, unafraid,
like the Capuchin friars who loved the beauty
in bones and nailed them to chapel walls—

decorative motifs of triangles and circles,
frescoes, columns, and arches, and suspended
from ceilings, filigree of lacey bones, shades

muting the light, a chimeless clock of vertebrae,
foot bones, and finger bones, its single hand
not marking time—all final remains of friars

asleep for years, exhumed and preserved
for beauty's sake—six rooms on the Via Veneto,
each underground and airless as a coffin,

in this room, skulls, in that, pelvises, and there,
leg bones and thigh bones, in that room, skeletons
reassembled, dressed in ancient robes,

and mounted to the wall like butterflies. No blanket
of green, no lilies or roses. *Memento mori* of bones,
singing seduction, our ears tilted towards the song.

August 11: Morning Prelude

Outside, a chorus of birds,
not bobolinks, but yellow-rumped warblers,
and the cooing of mourning doves, mated for life.

Inside, a man I love in the shower,
the rush of water, low hum of his lather and scrub,
his unbird-like music.

What I hope for: A day green as new-minted
money. No harm to my children.
My friend's illness not cancer.
The air clean and fresh as a man after a shower.

I make a plan: Ginger tea.
A lined tablet. Something in my head
gushing like a geyser.

Later: A reliable car.
A blue road.
A lodestar.

Beyond the road, on one side, sunflowers,
their faces baked brown and bonneted in yellow,
like children in costumes dancing in a field
buzzing with bumblebees.

On the other side, row after row of corn,
each stalk erect and watching the children.
The sky above blue and all around
the breathable air, fresh as soap.

The Seasons of a Long Marriage

Now that the sun angles past noon,
it shines through the glass doors.
And though I've squeegeed them
twice in two days, smudges
show on the other side.
Some spots just can't be removed.
They're here forever. Like scars.
Still, I can see squirrels scrambling
for nuts and fall's last leaves
fallen. The broken bones of trees.
Yesterday six deer grazed
the grass and munched stiff brown pods
dropped from locust trees.
The bird feeders are gone for the winter.
No more goldfinches this year,
those flashing fragments of sun.
Soon the green ground will be covered
with snow. The days turn cold.
My husband's hair is gray.

Losing Daylight

It's Sunday, 8th of November,
    sky gray as ashes, fall sliding
        into winter. Braced by wind

    and leaves, starlings glide
  like a flung blanket. I pour
another cup of tea, watch

a sheet of darkness land
    and lift, land and lift. After
        each departure, I breathe again.

    Last night, one more goodbye,
  the wind gaining force, rain
sheeting against the windows.

We spoke of failed efforts,
    the cauldron of hope and
        grief. Outside, summer's final

    flowers capitulated to the cold.
  This morning, the yard like a
graveyard, bodies exposed.

A boy's car radio, cranked up
    full-blast, shakes the street,
        reminds us of the strange dance

    of time, how it moves like a river,
  snaking and drifting away. The old
songs come back in waves of sorrow,

sorrow for our lost youth, our
        prodigal boy. While we slept or
                didn't, time shifted. The impatiens

                tumbled in their pots, the stalks
        like melted jelly. Our birch bends
over the grass. Just the two of us

here but not the same, stumbling
        through our days, two birds blown
                off-course, whirling, darkening

                the sky, grass, everything inside
        this house. We understand
prophecy now, the fallacy

of the parable's ending. We
        anticipate another night of rain,
                the earth wet, but not washed clean.

Morning Walk

Three times around the pond, three times
I cursed the cake that failed to rise, three times
the sun for its fidelity to the sky, and the swans

for their regal, arrogant necks.
Down the path beyond the pond, I cursed the dogs—
a black Labrador long past retrieving anything

and the absurd dachshund that reminded me
of my brother's little sausage dog, vanished
years ago, but not the sound of my brother's grief,

and farther down the path, five small boys
on a jungle gym. Of course, I cursed them,
cursed them hard because I know that one of five—

the one with curly hair—will someday disappear.
I cursed the swings and the babies being pushed,
their love of flight, arms flapping like birds' wings,

hands already waving *goodbye, goodbye*.
I cursed their mothers, still unbroken.
And then I cursed the tulips, purple hyacinths,

crocuses, each yellow daffodil
with its loud trumpet, its false message.
And the sky, that too, for the purity of its blue.

Four

Eminent Domain

It was the color of leather, dark brown like her belt,
thick as gravy and mottled—a dog, large and terrifying,
lying on the grass like a pile of leaves, one eye closed,
the other trained on her like the aperture of a camera,
territorial, a king come to claim this patch of earth,

a smear of blood across its mouth as if a painter
had dabbed there. She dared not move or raise
a hand and hoped it would not lunge. Beyond the dog,
a bundle of white fur, ruined, blood-spattered—
her child's rabbit, pink eyes wide, surprised by death.

Slowly she removed her belt, wrapped it around her fist,
buckle end in palm, as her father had done, and whipped
the dog, again and again, made it whimper and cry,
then untwirled the leather and struck with the buckle
until the dog ran, its fur streaked with blood.

The rabbit she scooped up in her arms,
carried him as if he were a sleeping infant
into the woods, buried him under a pile of leaves,
and returned to the hutch, its latch already lifted.
She removed the carrots, the bed of straw, the water,

and waited for hours on the porch, a mother at last,
waiting to explain to her child that sometimes what we love
goes away and doesn't come back. She would not speak
of revenge, how it had seized her, how good it had felt,
knowing she could split a boulder with her fist.

The Third Egg

Far from woodland or savanna, a rafter
of wild turkeys, at least a dozen in my yard,
their black bellies and iridescent wings

glistening in sunlight. Behind the glass,
I sat still and watched, repulsed
by the fleshy caruncles across each head,

the jiggly red wattles and dangling rope-like
flaps of skin on the throat,
and from the center of the breast, a tuft

of small feathers that had failed to grow.
They waddled and strutted and swiveled
their long necks like periscopes.

They dipped their beaks into the bird bath,
investigated the feeders, and foraged
the ground for seeds and nuts.

They cast long, dark shadows.
Two hens moved away from the group
and poked the piles of dead leaves, as if

looking for something they'd lost.
The biggest gobbler looked in at me.
I heard his low-pitched drumming noise.

He was not afraid, but I clutched my belly,
beating with child, this time my last hope.
I prayed hard that these feathered creatures

were no omens or portents, just birds on a stroll.
After they left, I searched outside for a feather,
an amulet for the seed blooming inside me.

Preservation

Cover the mirrors as in a house
where there's been a death,
each mirror shrouded in white cloth,
like the unused furniture
in an old English mansion
the owners can no longer maintain.

Let the mirrors remain only in the one room
visitors browse, their tickets in hand
as if entering a museum
to see how others once lived.

Still the pendulum's swing,
turn back the hands of the clock.
Let it be yesterday.

It's not Sylvia's terrible fish I fear, old age
slapping around on the floor.
It's not the cracks, the crazed glass,
or the distortions.

Stack all the mirrors in that one room,
the one I won't go in, the one that once was his.
Lock the door.
Keep the silver from leaking out.
Let me browse only among the portraits
and the barren flowerpots.

By the side of the road

a doorknob nestled in the weeds.
Maybe some trucker from Home Depot
had lightened his load or a careless shopper
tossed it out with her coffee cup.

The knob was brass, perfectly new and beautiful,
its surface etched and grooved,
something you could hold in your hand
and go where you wanted to go.

It glinted like a pile of gold
encircled by dandelions and clover,
as if held hostage or in a ritual ceremony
of praise or protection, a small god at the center.

I wondered what home now lacked
entrance or exit,
its residents forever permanent,
its guests forever uninvited—

maybe somebody's mother stuck inside,
pouring another drink while she waits
for the guest who won't arrive.
Maybe it was her hand the doorknob flew out of.

Maybe that knob wasn't lost at all,
but running away,
not wanting to go where she was headed,
not to that house,

its secrets hiding like demons in corners
and crouched under beds,
its girl poised like Cerberus outside the door,
her teeth bared, her fists empty and clenched.

The Light Sets the Record Straight

I am not what you see the moment before death.
I do not offer a last-minute epiphany.
I come with no reprieve.
Take the oil on your feet, the cross on your forehead.
I will not comfort you.
I will flicker, dim, and vanish.
Welcome the dark embrace.
I will never be mistaken for my evil twin.
I am my evil twin.
I am the absence of color, more dangerous than the whale.
Without me, no shadows.
Do not look for me at the end of a tunnel.
Do not expect me to get you there.
I am what comes days after being lost in the mine.
Pray that the canary lives.
I am the idea in your brain.
I contain a city.
I fill a room.
I am full of tricks, a protean shape-shifter.
Trapped in a glass, I leak out.
Raise the blinds, I seep in.
I can blind you if I've a mind to.
Find me in the eyes of your lover.
Years later, watch me disappear.
Beware my touch, so subtle you barely feel it.
So powerful, I can sink or save ships at sea.
Make of me what you will, I can bear it.
False flatterer, I can make you beautiful.
I can make you ugly.
I can utterly beguile you.
I can make you confess to crimes you never meant to commit.

Why I Read True Crime Books

It always happens in someone else's house,
the silence, the window lifted, lock broken,
children asleep, mother and father in bed,
a stranger mounting the stairs,
a gun, a baseball bat, an axe in hand,
someone else's final hour.

It's always someone else's family, not ours.
It's down the street, across town, not in our house.
I'm merely pushing off my father's hand.
I'm still intact, unbroken.
It's not my crackhead boyfriend creeping up the stairs
to slaughter my parents in their bed.

In the book it's always someone else's bed,
someone else's dreams fractured, someone else's horror.
That's not me flying down the stairs.
The ghosts that live forever live in that other house.
It's their bones, their lives, their illusions broken.
In my house it's just pages turned by hand.

It's not my father's hands
lifting the sleeping child out of bed,
not my family left behind forever broken,
no complicated ligatures to unravel in the morning hours,
no blood spatter on the walls of my house,
not my name wailed by the mother crumpled on the stairs,

not my mother, her eyes raw and glazed, who stares
into the camera, covers her face with both hands,
thinks of nothing but her child locked in a pervert's house,
locked in a closet with a makeshift bed.
It's them, not me counting down the first 48 hours,
terrified this case won't ever be broken.

I'm neither the mother nor the child who's broken.
My father wears a suit, carries a briefcase down the stairs,
doesn't dig in the desert for hours,
doesn't bury bodies in acres of sand.
He kisses me good-night and goes back to his bed.
He plants pink tulips and yellow daffodils behind our house.

I won't be broken by the book in my hands.
That vacant stare, the mayhem, the empty bed,
all theirs, not ours the grief in that flowerless house.

My New Boyfriend Covers Me Like a Floral Scarf

He wraps himself
around me, tucks me
inside his jeans, all

slim legs and authentic
fit. My skin of pima
cotton, his shameless

chambray. Oh, V-neck!
Scoopneck! Boatneck!
Most precious marled

sweater, he comes
in colors—aubergine,
marine, marmalade—

and just as my father
forewarned, I am ruined
by cashmere. Snug around

my waist like a filigree belt,
and his leggings, Sweet
Lord, they stretch. He slides

me into a cami, bedecked
in lace. Cascading color
block tunic, draped dolman

sleeve shirt, perfection
of elliptical cardigan. Even
my soft-pleat skirt. He slips

into my drawers, soft
and silken, encircles
my neck, covers me

in blossoms, down to my
snake-embossed feet.
Look, I am style in bloom.

Your Beard, I Love It Not

> *I could not endure a husband with a beard*
> *on his face: I had rather lie in the woolen.*
> —Much Ado About Nothing, 2.1.29-31

You say you want to marry me. You pant and paw
and whisper your desire, but I cannot betroth
myself to a man with a squirrel's tail ear to ear.

In ancient India, man's beard was sacred, but for
licentiousness—such as yours—would have been
publicly cut off. I only ask to shear you privately.

I will not to marriage admit impediments—no bush
to leap over, no border to cross, no Rubicon to chin
and cheek, no baffle before what might feed me.

Take a blade and hack it off—that birdless nest,
that crumb catcher, chinful of tumbleweed, duck
blind, lice hotel, that bugaboo of children, that pile
of leaves I dare not dive into.

You hope to achieve the look of a philosopher,
but Aristotle knew that *the beard does not make*
the sage. You are no Aristotle, but, like him,
clean-shaven must be.

Propose marriage, but no substitute for your beard—
no goatee, royale, monkey tail, or doorknocker.
If you and I are to wed, I want you naked and pink
as a newborn mouse.

Not for a moment, Lorca once said to Whitman,
have I failed to see your beard full of butterflies.
That was a beautiful thing to say, but mere flattery.

More likely what fluttered in that long white beard
were leaves of lettuce dribbled from Whitman's
dinner salad. I would not nibble there.

Come now and, with your heart, pledge to me
that sacred beard and let me cut it off. Let me be
your Delilah, lost in the wild field of your face.

Untying the Knot: A Sonnenizio

Let me not to the marriage of true minds
admit that what lies between us is not love
but merely something physical. No platonic knot
immaterially binds us, wedding mind to mind. Not for us

the lure of two eggheads nodding at breakfast,
The Times spread between us, coffee hot and laced
with hazelnut, our souls transcending last night's tumble.
We grasp only what can be touched. Purity's not for us.

We embrace the corporeal, admit nothing
of old age, no knuckles knobbed and arthritic,
nor our two ring fingers encircled with silly love knots.
We cherish each wild indiscretion, fear not the body's

hungers, only its decline, and regret not
the broken promises, but seize the flesh and fret not.

For the Chocolate Tasters

who sit around all day eating bonbons,
whose mission is to empty each fluted cup,
day after day in pursuit of the perfect truffle,

whose nights are filled with dreams of ganache,
who do not count calories or fret the heart
attack, diabetes, or cavities, but push forward

to the next confection, who make a virtue
of falling to temptation, these epicureans
of chocolate, who never say I've had enough,

but like Olympic athletes persevere and savor
the literal taste of sweet success, who worship
the chocolatiers as they would gods and study

the science of chocolate, how to hold up a piece
to the light, to inspect for sheen and the slight
fissure, how to snap it and listen for the crack

that signals perfection, how to soften a Belgian
treat with the teeth and not chew, who train
like sommeliers to master the bunny sniff,

to breathe in the aroma notes, and show up
at work each day with a whiff of expectation,
who practice the fine art of slow eating,

grateful for each one of the 8000 taste buds
on the tongue, the hypersensitive palate,
steadfast in their refusal to rush joy.

A Polemic for Pink

I've bowed down before scarlet, worshipped
the green of fresh-minted money, and gravitated
towards black. I've lived in the absence of color.

So many times I've praised the whiteness of my pet
rat's fur, the red beads of his eyes, but never
the pink of his tail, naked and squiggly
like a worm and just as pink.

Consider the universality of the tongue,
the spot where we are all equal—and pink.
I've been licked by a cat's pink tongue, rough
as sandpaper, the small engine of his body whirring.

Remember the colors of terror—
red, orange, yellow, blue, and green—colors
that told us how afraid we needed to be.
Not one of them Code Pink.

Why would a rock star call herself Pink if it weren't
outrageous, her body half naked on a trapeze,
her hair pink as cotton candy?

I like a color that dares to be outrageous, but doesn't
mind going soft and pink as a watered-down communist,
that eschews the ideological red of marinara
for the creamy compromise of pink sauce.

I've loved a girl in a pink tutu, the way she rose up
on pink satin shoes and twirled around and around,
circles of pink spinning out a galaxy.

I've tapped my psychedelic foot to the music
of Pink Floyd, opened my heart to the little pink houses
of America, and fallen to temptation in a pink Cadillac.

Imagine spring without pink. No more blossoms
of magnolia dropped like ladies' hankies on the lawn.
No more borders of snapdragons lined up like pink pacifists.
No more the widow's consolation of pink gladiolas.

I've sunk my teeth into the crisp skin
of a Pink Lady, drenched my own poisonous flesh
in a lotion of utopian pink and let it conciliate the itch.

Don't call pink a wimp. Think about the power
of a pink slip, strong enough to shatter a life.
The ache of a pink ribbon, worn where a breast used to be.

And Jackie Kennedy in the back of a black
Lincoln Continental, her pink Chanel suit like a drift
of blossoms blown across her husband's body.

Five

An Epistemology of Promiscuity

I doused the tree and the feeder
      that dangled from it (the one
            you'd hung before you left),
doused them with
      hot pepper sauce
           to keep the squirrels away.

        I needed to do this.

      They'd leapt and flown from tree
    to feeder, gnawed the metal guards,
and stolen the seeds.

After the spraying, they scattered
      and stared from afar,
          inching closer and closer,
              circling the base of the tree,
    debating the risk—was it worth it,
the burning tongue, the itching eyes?

      It must have stirred desire, to see
  a swarm of finches
at the feeder and receive only
      the occasional
           dropped seeds, to squat
    like street beggars,
cups extended for the plink of a coin.

    They danced like bacchanals,
        bit each other with their sharp teeth,
            and went insane.

           They performed lewd
      sexual acts as if
to satisfy one hunger

might satisfy another, sniffing
        the air for sunflower chips, cracked
            corn, diced peanuts,
                    and pushing harder,
        pushing faster, taking
what they could get to fill
            the aching cup.

In My Yard, the Bones of Trees

I want sturdy oak trees, elms, and hickories,
but not the fallen leaves,
raked into grave-like mounds of debris.

Trees have hearts and this is how they grieve—
by letting go of what's already gone,
baring their arms in quiet bereavement.

Like a marriage scraped to the bone
and stripped of tender flesh,
the color's leached, the hearts petrified to stone.

Arms and hearts flailed and thrashed,
cast off what had desiccated and grown cold,
changing what once was lovely into trash.

Trees take back what arms could not hold—
in spring, like love as new invention,
they retrieve what winter stole.

For us, no such chance at regeneration.
While our trees regain what they've lost,
we could not repair the final disintegration,

so wished each other luck and quietly divorced.
The morning of your leaving,
our arms fell empty, the two of us bereft.

Sinkholes

One morning someone's husband leaves
for work and never returns. Or someone's

cousin takes a trip to Mexico and crosses
the border there's no crossing back over.

Or maybe your daughter heads to school
but never arrives. Alice down the rabbit hole,

forever in freefall. Sometimes they disappear
like that, one by one,

sometimes by the hundreds, the thousands.
Strangers. People we've loved. Poof!—

like rabbits stuffed back in the hat.
Today the earth opened up and sucked in

a man's bedroom—the man asleep on his
lumpy mattress, his sad erotic dreams

down into a mystery of limestone and sand.
Gone the vertical cracks in the tiles, the slight

shifting of walls, the popping creaks at night.
Only a hole where his room used to be, as if

the earth, like a Titan, had eaten her child.
The neighbors throw flowers into the crater—

lilies, orchids, red hibiscus. They build a shrine.
Someone adds a bench, a place for the mother

to sit and grieve. A place to pray.
Dear Lord, give me something to bury. A piece

of his shirt, a fragment of bone, a strand of his hair.

Your Blue Shirt

Left behind like a cicada shell,
it hangs, so incredibly
blue. I slip into it, wear it like skin,
the body I loved all over me—
my breasts, my back, my neck—
your scent in the weave.
All day I breathe you in,
put off the final disrobing.

Where Feathers Go When They Fall

All night, dreams of birds
    and flight. Tickled awake,
        my mouth fills with feathers,

        blue jay, warbler, starling.
    I yawn and breathe, inhalation
of air and feathers. Blue sky

pulls me to the window.
    Arms folded at the elbow
        flap and flap like wings.

        I balance on the ledge,
    tumble and glide into blue.
Morning scurries by

on two clawed feet. Head
    bobbing, beak pecking
        green blades—a strange

        new appetite for worms,
    and oh, delight! I consume
and consume. Outside

the house where I once lived,
    I build a nest of silken floss
        and tiny twigs, watch the lives

        on the other side, and bless
    this freedom. Home is a tree
now, children hatched

and gone, none to peck
    my heart. I do not worry
        or grieve, only imagine them

                in tall trees, too high for
        cat's paw, and go back
to fumbling for worms.

My trills and tweets, pitch
        perfect, fill the air with song.
                I ruffle the forsythia, azalea,

        andromeda, dip into
the bath and splash off
the long winter, shaking

my multi-colored plumage,
        not one feather of cardinal,
                scarlet bird bound for life,

        such binding once
will suffice. The love
I have is for the daffodils.

Coloring

Rose was the color of her cheeks,
skin thin as sausage casing,
so precise with her rouge
as was the girl with her crayons

lined up in a box of symmetry,
their lovely points to outline and color her trees,
her mountains, and sun,

until the hideous art teacher
crept up beside her and with ringless fingers
broke magenta,

snapped it in half,
and used the side of one piece
to shadow and shade.

It was a kind of beginning,
to hate someone so deeply,
someone who could break the beauty
of magenta.

Many times in the days after,
she was offered crimson, scarlet, purple,
but the spot inside her that had loved magenta—
now a cistern of grief.

Not ever in the years that followed
would love be that fierce,
never again the sun that intense.

The Morning After

The sun wasn't where it was supposed to be,
wasn't up when it should have been up,
      and couldn't have been down—
      too early for that,

early enough that the goldfinches
should have been singing
      and they were there perched
      in the evergreens but not

singing, not flying beneath the blue sky,
the sky so blue it must have been morning
      and the doves, as if to prove they knew
      what mourning meant, stopped

cooing. She was still breathing,
alive to the wind, the cold on her skin,
      cold yet summer still.
      And the roses, in aftershock, froze

their petals and silenced the beetles
and bees in the pistils. No buzzing now
      as they circled her head,
      and above her no sun, no heat, no song

from the birds, no attar in the air, and what,
she wondered, had happened to the sun,
      the reliable sun that never failed
      to show up, but today hadn't

shown up, leaving her
like the woman who reaches for a peach
      but finds only an empty branch,
      the tree barren, the sun gone from the sky.

Pity the Poor Fortune Cookie Writer His Muse

All day at his desk tapping out lines of good
cheer, ten words or less to stave off despair,
before him a widower, wife dead for a month,
that man now among good-hearted neighbors
sharing their Sunday night Chinese take-out.

After the House Lo Mein, the Almond Chicken,
and a Vegetable Roll with enough cabbage
to disturb his slumber for a week, he cracks
open the clam shell of his tasteless cookie
and pulls out his fortune: *Life is beautiful,*

be happy. Like the man so sick with flu he can't
believe he will ever be well again, he thinks,
Impossible. And suddenly he is weeping fat
salty tears into the leftover Moo Goo Gai Pan.
His friends, observing his grief, pass him a more

congenial cookie: *Even a small gift brings joy
to the whole family.* His tears run like the Yangtze.
One more cookie crosses over the Chow Mein
congealing in its white cardboard box: *A fresh start
will put you on your way.* And another: *A smile*

is your personal welcome mat. In their little
waxed paper bag the crispy fried noodles turn
to ashes as cookies are lobbed like baseballs:
A light heart carries you through the hard times.
How he wishes he could believe *The best path*

is always the hardest one, that he could *Accept
what cannot be changed.* The bite of pineapple
on his tongue, he remembers the last time the two
of them shared Chinese at the Golden Mountain,
weeks before her illness, a platter of Dragon

and Phoenix between them, and Seven Stars
with Moon, the fortune she'd unraveled: *True gold
fears no fire*, how easy it was then to believe
the golden egg of happiness had fallen into his lap.

Signs

To find yourself in the park on the very day
all the dogs stayed home, surely, that's a sign.

To trust once more in the greenness of grass,
that the blades will not cut you. To believe

that the stony path leads somewhere, not nowhere,
and is not a metaphor for your heart, that a soft

rabbit still lives inside you and after its long sleep
rubs its pink eyes, rises, and brings you back

to the park. To stand beside the playground
to gaze at the giant concrete turtle, without hating

the young mothers whose children climb across
its capacious back. To release the string that's held

you tight as a noose and watch the balloon of sorrow
float into the blue sky and disperse like helium.

To know that the brook babbles again for you,
that purple hyacinths blossom unbruised this year—

violets, lilacs, wisteria, too—that the turtle is now
your emblem, and if you're lucky, which you are,

those you have shut out, those you have hurt
with the hard shell of your silence will somehow

still love you and you will move towards them,
carrying the ancient notched shell, your back

uncrushed by its weight, the mystery
of its hieroglyphics unfolded and laid at their feet.

And Life Goes On As It Has Always Gone On

Snow and then more of it and just when spring
seems possible, a blizzard leaves you powerless.
Your flowers in bud expire.
Children ring your doorbell and disappear.
Late at night, when you can't sleep, the TV asks,
Do you know where your children are?
and you say, *No,* or *Yes, in jail.*
Bees build nests under the eaves of your house.
They hunt you down and stab you many times
with their tiny switchblades—even your lips
while you're eating a ham sandwich.
Blinded by an armful of fresh towels, you fall
down the stairs while rushing to answer the phone.
Your vertebrae shattered, that call from your lover
forever unanswered, sex forever impossible.
Something hurts your heart—an odd balloon
in your chest, poofing and unpoofing,
days in the hospital hooked up to machines,
then a diet stripped of cakes and pies.
In Greece poppies cover the islands in spring,
scarlet flowers waving like silk scarves.
People in kouzinas eat poppy seed cakes
and speak of Demeter, how she devoured
the black seeds to fall asleep and forget
her grief over the loss of her daughter.
Outside your window, spring arrives flowerless.
Crackheads move in next door.
Your dog dies from a poisoned meatball.
Are you looking for compensation?
A rabbit nibbling the grass—does that console?
Does ice cream suffice? even if served
with marshmallow fluff? Delicious, but is it enough
as you lie in your hospital bed plugged to a monitor
and dreaming of sex, the little red pumping
machine of your heart opening like a poppy in bloom?

Acknowledgments

Grateful acknowledgment is made to the following journals in which some of the poems in this collection first appeared.

Avatar Review: "August 11, Morning Prelude," "In Defense of the Cashew," "I Want to Save the Trees," "The Light Sets the Record Straight"
burntdistrict: "And Life Goes On As It Has Always Gone On"
Cider Press Review: "The Morphology of Mushrooms"
Compose: "The Gift of a Rat," "We Were Such a Fine Plum Pudding"
Connotation Press: "Knot-Tying," "Pity the Poor Fortune Cookie Writer His Muse," "A Polemic for Pink," "Two-Door Mailbox with Gin," "Untying the Knot: A Sonnenizio," "Why I Read True Crime Books"
The Cortland Review: "Shopping at the Short Hills Mall"
Driftless: "Thinking Like a Buddhist"
Innisfree Poetry Journal: "Your Blue Shirt," "The Wrong Monkey"
Ithaca Lit: "Where Feathers Go When They Fall," "'Why yellow makes me sad'"
Journal of New Jersey Poets: "Losing Daylight"
Kestrel: "My New Boyfriend Covers Me Like a Floral Scarf," "Your Beard, I Love It Not"
Little Patuxent Review: "After"
Mezzo Cammin: "In My Bones," "In My Yard, the Bones of Trees," "My Arty *Ars Poetica*: A Cento"
Mojave River Review: "Coloring," "For the Love of Avocados," "How I Dumped You," "The Instincts of a Dog"
Mom Egg: "Nesting"
Naugatuck River Review: "Original Sin," "Warnings"
Poet Lore: "Preservation"
Prime Number: "By the side of the road"
The Quotable: "The Morning After"

Rose Red Review: "The Color of Magic"
Southern Poetry Review: "For the Chocolate Tasters," "Morning Walk"
The Stillwater Review: "All Night Awake, My Innards Gone Awry," "The Phone Call"
Tahoma Literary Review: "Signs"
Thrush: "Dreaming to Lionel Richie's 'Dancing on the Ceiling'"
Tiferet: "The Seasons of a Long Marriage"
Valparaiso Poetry Review: "How Heavy the Snow," "Sinkholes," "Sweet Images"
Waccamaw: "The Third Egg"
Weave Magazine: "The Pull of Bones"

"For the Love of Avocados" and "My New Boyfriend Covers Me Like a Floral Scarf" were reprinted in *Serving House Journal.*

"Why I Read True Crime Books" was reprinted in *Obsessions: Sestinas in the Twenty-First Century*, edited by Carolyn Beard Whitlow and Marilyn Krysl (UPNE, 2014).

"Original Sin" won the First Place Prize in the 2012 *Naugatuck River Review* contest.

About the Author

Diane Lockward is the author of *The Crafty Poet: A Portable Workshop* (Wind Publications, 2013) and three earlier poetry books, most recently *Temptation by Water*. Her previous books are *What Feeds Us*, which received the 2006 Quentin R. Howard Poetry Prize, and *Eve's Red Dress*. She is also the author of two chapbooks, *Against Perfection* and *Greatest Hits: 1997-2010*. Her poems have been included in such anthologies as *Poetry Daily: 360 Poems from the World's Most Popular Poetry Website* and Garrison Keillor's *Good Poems for Hard Times*, and in such journals as *Harvard Review*, *Spoon River Poetry Review*, and *Prairie Schooner*. Her work has also been featured on *Poetry Daily*, *Verse Daily*, and *The Writer's Almanac*.

www.ingramcontent.com/pod-product-compliance
Lightning Source LLC
Chambersburg PA
CBHW021132300426
44113CB00006B/389